THE BOOK OF BLAISE

A Saint and his Name

Also by this author:

Bloomington Days: Town and Gown in Middle America

Cathedrals of Learning: Great and Ancient Universities of Western Europe

Stickmen: Reflections on the Goalie's Eccentric Art

B-town Blues

Westported

Beached

Hewn from Yew: Newry Notables Past and Present

Fiction:

The Fake's Progress: A Fragmentary Account of the Early Life of Sebastian Conyers

The Fake's Regress: Further Fragments from the Life of Sebastian Conyers

The Fake's Egress: Yet Further Fragments from the Life of Sebastian Conyers

The Fake's Success: Some Remaining Fragments from the Life of Sebastian Conyers

THE BOOK OF BLAISE

A Saint and his Name

Blaise Cronin

PublishNation LLC
www.publishnation.net

Contents

Name that child   1

Who was Saint Blaise?   11

Blaise goes global   23

Celebrating Blaise   33

Blaise's bits and bobs   39

Representations of Blaise   43

Coda   51

Image credits   55

About the author   57

NAME THAT CHILD

What's in a name? Quite a lot, when you think about it. Our given names tag us for life. We can't escape them, well not easily. (Family names, too: who'd want to be called Mr. Stalin or Ms. Goebbels?) In the eyes of others, we are our name. Be it James or Judy, Petronella or Peregrine, it becomes a shorthand for all that we have said and done, a near unique identifier: 'Oh, Judy, well, you know what Judy's like.' Marked and parked, as classificationists like to say. Of course, not all names are created equal. Many come with baggage, tainted in the popular mind with venal or perfidious acts: Adolf and Osama have lost their appeal in certain though by no means all sections of society. Some names are euphonious, others dull to the ear—no names, no pack-drill. Nor are names neutral. As surveys show, some are deemed classier than others, signaling membership of a particular socio-economic group: 'Hooray Henrys,' braying upper-crust English males, being a case in point. If one girl is named Arabella and another Sharon, we have a pretty good idea of their respective social origins. Others, such as made-up names, may suggest membership of a lower caste or affiliation with a particular ethnic or racial group. With the flick of a switch a fine name, Frederick, can be rendered a trifle plodding: Fred. Diminutives, cute and convenient though they be, sometimes diminish a name. Occasionally, however, it works in reverse, as when now dated Gertrude is shortened to the lighter, more fashionable Trudy. But there's no stopping our fondness for diminutives, such is the value we place on both speed and informality in contemporary society. Al is so much easier than Aloysius, Max than Maximilian.

Like hemlines and hair length, a name's appeal may rise and fall with the times. Popularity charts will tell you whether your name is among the 1,000 most popular; whether it has broken into the top twenty in the last few years. But as your nominal stock rises, your name's exclusivity declines. Some of us would prefer that our given name held on to its low ranking. In a crowded room, a hollered 'John' will produce more hands than a shouted 'Blaise.' Do Johns and Marys, I wonder, every grow tired of being introduced to other Johns and Marys? In contemporary Britain, the most common name for boys (when variant spellings are combined) is Muhammed. Imagine the forest of hands if a teacher in a Birmingham or Bradford school asks, 'Is Muhammed present?' Growing up in provincial Ulster, I rather enjoyed my nominal uniqueness and experienced a sense of diminishment when I discovered that I was no longer the only Blaise in town.

In that benighted province, names have long been indicative of tribal allegiance: Conor and Sean are likely to be Catholics/Nationalists (left-footers in local parlance), Robert and Albert, Protestants/Unionists (right-footers). During 'the Troubles' your physical wellbeing could depend on your parents' choice of name: Blaise flummoxed most bigots. But while names may signify class, religious or ideological ties, there has also been a marked shift of late to nominal classlessness, not to mention whimsy. Your child may be the apple of your eye, but is that reason enough to call your daughter after a piece of fruit? If you're a movie actress and life-style entrepreneur and your ex-husband a musician, then the answer is yes. But to be fair, if a girl can be baptized Daisy, Violet or Iris, what is the logical objection to moving from flowers to fruit? One could argue, after all, that in western Europe, the apple is at the core of Christian iconography, a symbol of lost Edenic life, not to mention a recurring trope in folklore. And don't forget that New York is known affectionately as the Big Apple while the world's most famous personal computer is…the Apple.

Setting the bar high in the celebrity naming stakes, Bob Geldof called his daughter Peaches Honeyblossom, a heady mix of fruit and flower. Surely it is but a matter of time before some poor sod is named Turnip or Banana, though probably not in France where Strawberry (*Fraise*) has already been banned:

other names nixed by the French courts were Nutella and Mini Cooper. In the UK, Martian and Money are among those to have been rejected by the registrar's office. Different nations and states have different rules for naming children and common sense does not always prevail. A US judge's attempt to ban the name Messiah failed: the Second Coming was recorded by officialdom in the state of Tennessee. Of course, when it comes to nicknames all is fair play: Spud and Ginger are staples of Irish vernacular.

Before considering the origins of the name Blaise—one inextricably associated with the most popular of the three Catholic saints bearing that name, that is to say, the Armenian who was martyred in the fourth century—it is worth noting how a traditionally and resolutely male name has in recent years been given to, or been appropriated by, a relatively small number of females. A survey of births for Blaise (and its variants) in England and Wales for the period 1996-2014 reveals that Blaise, Blaze and Blaize have all been recorded for both males and females, with the traditional spelling being the most popular in each case. The highest number of registered births in any one year for Blaise was 18 (males) with Blaze (males again) in second place. In no given year did either variant break into the thousand most popular names in the country. As far as the US is concerned, the name was almost unheard of until the 1990s, with no more than a couple of hundred registered each year thereafter. In France, Blaise is a long-established Christian name, not reserved for just boys but also affixed to villages, communes, streets, churches, shops and wine (Ch. La Tour Saint Blaise from Bordeaux) (see illus.1). A river, la Blaise, has given its name to Courcelles-sur-Blaise, Vaux-sur-Blaise, Blaisy and Lachapelle-en-Blaisy, amongst others. In the UK, the name is not unheard of; Blaise Castle, an 18th-century folly, is in Bristol, part of the Blaise Castle Estate, home to the Blaise Toy Museum. In the center of Bromley, Kent, you'll find St. Blaise's Well, former site of a medieval church bearing the saint's name (illus.2). No doubt the well's water has, or once had, curative properties. Up north in Bradford, there is a St. Blaise Court and St. Blaise Way:

in pre-Industrial Revolution times St. Blaise's Day mattered nearly as much to the denizens of that city as Christmas Day, for reasons that will be explained later. In 1222, Oxford council forbade all servile work on the good saint's feast day. The parish and town of St. Blazey in Cornwall are also named after the miracle-worker from Armenia. Each year his feast day is celebrated with a lantern parade, featuring an illuminated ram, through the streets of the small town. Formerly, the occasion was marked with bonfires atop English hills and celebrations in places such as Norwich and Saffron Walden. In Merrie England, his memory endures.

Time was most people in a word association test would link the name with either the popular Catholic saint or the celebrated 17th-century French mathematician and philosopher, Blaise Pascal. A few might conceivably mention Robert de Boron's 12th-century epic, *Merlin*, in which Blaise, a holy man, acts as a companion and chronicler to the wizard Merlin or, possibly, Thomas Malory's *Le Morte d'Arthur* in which my namesake appears as Bleise. Lovers of the turf might pipe up that St. Blaise won the Derby in 1883 before being shipped off to the US to stand as a stallion. Despite the fact that the name remains closely associated with St. Blaise and has been historically given to boys, these days it has become fashionable to treat Blaise as unisex. Google 'Blaise Pascal,' for example, and you may find yourself reading not about the Frenchman's famous wager but about a female singer/songwriter of that name from Toronto. Blaise does seem to be a name that appeals to those of musical bent. The Irish *chanteuse* Tara Blaise, born Tara Egan-Langley, presumably reckoned that re-branding herself as Blaise would pep up her career. During the Swinging Sixties, Blaises was a hip club in Queensgate, London, where the likes of Jimi Hendrix, Pink Floyd and Yes performed. In popular culture, the name was propelled into the limelight by the British comic strip (progenitor of several spin-off movies) featuring the voluptuous Modesty Blaise, from which, in due course, the celebrated English Burlesque dancer, Immodesty Blaize (a.k.a. Kelly Fletcher), took inspiration. No doubt, the name's cachet received a further boost

Illustration 1: French village and Parisian shop named 'Blaise.'

Illustration 2: St. Blaise's Well, Bromley, Kent.

with the appearance of Blaise Zabini, son of a witch and pupil at Hogwarts School, in J.K. Rowling's blockbuster *Harry Potter* series. By way of footnotes, in the world of chemistry the Blaise Reaction—reported for the first time in 1901—is named after the French chemist Edmond E. Blaise. In the 1980s, the name-as-acronym was used to promote the **B**ritish **L**ibrary **A**utomated **I**nformation **SE**rvice. By happy coincidence, the **BL** employed me in an advertising campaign for its online system: a nominal marriage of convenience, one might say (illus.3). It was also in the early 1980s that the late Ian Constantinides established his architectural conservation company St Blaise, whose projects included the restoration of Windsor Castle following the disastrous 1992 fire.

The gender-bending trend, whether one cares for it or not, is likely to continue as more naming sites choose to treat Blaise as if it were a unisex name. Certainly, in the US it can be a risky business guessing an individual's chromosome pairing based on given names: landmines include Avery, Jordan, Riley, Ryan and Taylor. Purists may raise eyebrows at the de-gendering trend, but it is probably a lost battle. As with spoken language, prescriptivists tend to get brushed aside by the relentless tide of common usage. Sometimes a name becomes less frequently associated with one sex and more with the other: a case in point is Evelyn. In the UK, the writer Evelyn Waugh was married to a woman called Evelyn Gardner. For purposes of disambiguation as much as amusement they were known in some quarters as He-velyn and She-evelyn. He pronounced his name as EEV-lin. Confusion was and may well still be understandable: a 2016 poll listed Waugh among the top-100 most read *female* authors in US college classes. In some cases, the adoption of a male-sounding name might be designed to fool the public intentionally, as with the 19th-century French writer George Sand, born Amantine Lucile Aurore Dupin, but there is nothing to suggest that a desire to deceive plays a part in the naming or self-naming of females as Blaise. Naming conventions, in any case, will continue to evolve.

Illustration 3: 1980s British Library promotional leaflet.

For the record, it should be noted that Blaise has also long functioned as a surname. In Middle Ages Britain it was more often used as a family name (in various forms) than a given name. Today, it is most commonly found in Africa, Chad in particular, but also in Haiti and a number of other countries: the sixth Prime Minister of Granada was one Herbert Augustus Blaize. Other local variants include Blais and Blasé. In France over the centuries, variants of the name have evolved reflecting regional cultural and linguistic differences: Blais, Blaies, Blay, de Blaise and Blaison being examples. Same story, too, in Italy, Spain and elsewhere.

WHO WAS SAINT BLAISE?

For most purposes and most people, the (given) name Blaise is synonymous with the third-century saint of that name. He is the first Blaise people—people of a certain generation at any rate—hear of. The name's origins, however, go back far in time. Blaise is the French and primary version of the ancient Roman cognomen, Blaesus, a cognomen being the third and usually last of the three names a citizen of Rome would have had. They functioned like descriptive nicknames—neutral or naughty rather than nice—and were passed down from father to son, in the process shedding their original *raison d'être*. (Eminent individuals were sometimes granted an honorific cognomen.) To take just one example, the cognomen of Marcus Tullius Cicero, the famous Roman statesmen and writer, stemmed from the Latin word for chickpea. It had nothing to do directly with the great orator, either personally or professionally, but derived from the fact that one of his ancestors had a cleft on the tip of his nose that purportedly resembled a chickpea. What Cicero thought of being reduced, nominally, to a chickpea must remain the subject of speculation. Other cognomens that would be familiar to any grammar school pupil include Brutus (heavy), Rufus (red-haired) and Blandus (charming).

Blaesus was one such cognomen. The meaning of the adjective was lisping, so Blaesus in its original usage denoted a person with a mild speech impediment. It would, however, be wrong to assume that someone granted that cognomen was an individual of little or no consequence: Quintus Julius Blaesus, for instance, was a military commander who became proconsul of Africa in the first century; Publius Sallustius Blaesus a Roman senator. It is quite unlikely that either man had much in common with Biggus Dickus, the lisping Roman nobleman in the Monty Python film *Life of Brian*. The meager historical record does not indicate whether Blaise himself was the lisper or an ancestor. Given that he would become known as a curer of sore throats, it is in either case slightly ironic. Over time, Blaesus morphed into Blasius, and it is by this late Latin form that St. Blaise (illus.4) would have been known during his lifetime.

In the pantheon of Catholic saints—numbering roughly 10,000—Blaise may not rank among the most elite or best known but he is far from an also-ran. Indeed, he is one of a small number of saints to appear in Michelangelo's 'The Last Judgment' (Sistine Chapel, Vatican), as a result of which he, at one point, achieved a certain notoriety. Dressed in red robe and holding a pair of wool combs, Blaise was originally shown looking down at buxom, bare-breasted Saint Catherine and her wheel. This did not sit well with the prudish Church hierarchy and several years later the work was repainted such that Catherine was appropriately clothed, and Blaise's lecherous-seeming gaze directed elsewhere. It was in the Middle Ages that his popularity soared, his reputation as a protector, healer and occasional miracle worker spreading across all parts of Europe and beyond, even to remote Iceland where he developed a near cult-like following. Over the centuries, his feast day has continued to be celebrated from Croatia to California, from Spain to Paraguay and he remains venerated not only in the Catholic Church but also in the Eastern Orthodox Church (the Orthodox Catholic Church) and Oriental Orthodox Church—his sanctification preceded the Great Schism of the 11th century. In folklore, literature and art he maintains a multi-faceted and enduring presence. Seventeen hundred years after his death, he is still garnering ink; a February 2020 Philippines newspaper article was headlined: 'Saint Blaise and the coronavirus' while a January 2021 piece in *The Dubrovnik Times* read, 'I'm sure that St. Blaise would navigate Covid-19 although maybe not Zoom.'

*Illustration 4: 'Saint Blasius,' 19th-century painting by
Antonio Molleno, Art Institute of Chicago.*

If Blaise could be reduced to a single dimension it would be his role as patron saint of children with sore throats, based on his having saved the life of a young boy choking on a fish bone. But, in fairness, it should be noted that he is not the only saint associated with otorhinolaryngology or ENT (ears, nose and throat). St. Godelina, an 11th-century Flemish martyr who was strangled to death, is also invoked in the case of throat ailments (and difficult marriages, hers being the very cause of her martyrdom). Such is the number of saints and the range of specialized intercession within their collective gift that the Church has someone on call for almost every conceivable illness or eventuality. Blaise, however, is no one-trick pony. For reasons that have become blurred with the passage of time he has been considered, variously, the saint of physicians, veterinarians, wax-handlers, plowmen, shepherds, wool combers and fisherfolk.

The *Ur* miracle performed by St. Blaise has guaranteed his fame and is sufficient to disambiguate him from the two other early saints with whom he shares a name: Blaise of Caesarea in Cappadocia, a shepherd, who suffered and died for his beliefs, and Blaise of Amorion, a pious ninth-century monk who spent time in both Rome and Constantinople. Neither one of these has much of a presence in church history or popular legend, though in England the notion prevailed in some quarters, notably the woolen trade, that Saint Blaise came from Jersey. That confusion may have arisen from the fact that Caesarea is Latin for Jersey. In any case, even when it comes to laying out more or less certifiable facts about the best known and by far most frequently invoked of the three Saints Blaise, one struggles to find the barest bones of a convincing narrative. The truth is that over the centuries a quite remarkable amount of legend and folklore has accreted around a rather exiguous factual base, something the Catholic Church acknowledges openly and refers to as 'popular piety.'

Blaise (or Blasius) was born in the episcopal city of Sebaste (Sebastea/Sebasteia), which corresponds to modern-day Sivas in lesser Armenia (now Turkey). Sebaste, as it was known during

14

the Roman Empire, was founded originally by Pompey the Great and likely called Megalopolis in its early days. For a period, it was an important settlement. Blaise's exact date of birth is unknown, but it was sometime in the third century and he likely died around 316, martyred on the orders of Agricolaus, governor of Cappadocia during the reign of Emperor Licinius (see illus.5). Even though the Edict of Toleration, granting freedom of religion, had been passed a few years earlier, the persecution of Christians continued in Armenia. It is probably wise, however, to preface every statement about Blaise's character, life and accomplishments with the phrase, 'Legend has it that...' The earliest mention of the sainted martyr and his signature miracle—the removal of the bone stuck in the child's throat—can be found in the medical writings of the sixth-century Byzantine Greek physician Aëtius Amidenus. Much later, in the 13th-century classic *Travels of Marco Polo*, there is passing mention of Sebaste, the city therein referred to as the place where 'Saint Blaise obtained the glorious crown of martyrdom.' Apart from these extremely slim pickings, we have little to go on bar the apocryphal *Acts of Saint Blaise*, written in Greek roughly four hundred years after his death.

Stories about the saint would have been handed down orally over the centuries and by the time they were recorded have undergone considerable embellishment. If swallowed whole, the mass of alleged miracles attributed to Blaise might just stick in the throat, necessitating the intervention of the good saint himself. Similar caution is warranted when reading accounts of his life in the *Golden Legend*, a collection of hagiographies, written by Jacobus Voragine, archbishop of Genoa, in the 13th century. These were translated into English and published more than a hundred years later by William Caxton. The words attributed to the saint are fanciful, the date of his death inaccurate. Similar caution is advised, too, in the case of Camillo Tutini's 17th-century account of Blaise's life, *Narratione della vita e miracoli di S. Biagio Vescovo e Martire*.

Illustration 5: 13th-century stained-glass window with Blaise and Agricolaus, Louvre, Paris.

Blaise's parents, it has been suggested, were of rich and noble stock and raised him as a Christian. Before being appointed Bishop of Sebaste at a relatively young age, he had a successful career as a physician, blessed with—the more colorful chroniclers of his life and times aver—wonderful healing powers. It is likely that he would have been nominated by the local community for the bishopric before being vetted and consecrated by the Church hierarchy. At some point, to avoid persecution for his beliefs, he fled to the countryside, or, alternatively, he responded to a call from God to lead the life of a hermit in—again depending on one's source—the woods, a ditch or a cave on Mount Argeos along with others fleeing persecution. There, rather like St. Francis of Assisi centuries later, he not only befriended wildlife but healed sick birds and animals, including a wolf. Whether by accident or design, Blaise was discovered by a group of the governor's hunters scouring the countryside and apprehended. It was while on his way to prison that the miracle-worker famously removed a fish bone from the throat of a small boy who was choking to death at his mother's side—the Heimlich maneuver *avant la lettre*? It is also claimed that he encountered another woman before his incarceration whose pig had been seized by a wolf. Blaise duly commanded the predator to return the animal. It obeyed and the terrified creature fell from the wolf's grip unhurt. Later, the pig owner would visit Blaise in prison, bringing him two candles to lessen the gloom of his cell. To this day a pair of crossed (sometimes lit) candles remain among the most frequently reproduced emblems of the saint. Another defining symbol is a wool comb, the reason for which will soon become clear.

Blaise was tortured at the order of Agricolus but would neither renounce his faith nor worship pagan idols. For refusing to apostatize, he was (possibly) thrown into a lake but, miraculously, the water either parted around him or he walked upon it, to the fury of his captor. Next, he was beaten then hung from on high (or laid out on a stone slab) and his flesh torn with iron carding combs. The recusant bishop was finally beheaded. His canonization took place long before the Roman Curia, in the shape of the Congregation for the Causes of Saints (founded in 1588), assumed exclusive authority for canonization and beatification. Saint Blaise is thus designated as pre-Congregation, having been elevated to the sainthood by a local bishop or primate, based, in all likelihood, on a critical mass of posthumous lore and popular devotion. Since then, the tools used to flay him alive have been reproduced in countless images in multiple media: paintings, icons, sculptures, murals, cards, medals, stained glass, postage stamps, and much more (see illus.6). They also explain why he became the patron saint of the wool trade in Middle Ages England and later a beloved figure in Bradford, center of the UK wool industry during its halcyon days, where his full-length statue still adorns the Gothic Revival Wool Exchange.

Over the centuries, Blaise's reputation grew and stories about his miraculous powers spread, most significantly during the Black Death, when he was one of a select group of saints known as the Fourteen Holy Helpers (*Vierzehnheiligen*), to whom the credulous turned for succor. The plague killed more than half of Europe's population and in place of vaccines the fearful looked to the Holy Helpers, each of whom possessed a particular God-given gift: St. George, for instance, was invoked for skin diseases and palsy; St. Cyriacus offered hope to those suffering from eye problems (or diabolic possession); St. Barbara was your insurance against fire and electric storms. Blaise, naturally, was the man to turn to for throat ailments…and protection of domestic animals. As his fame grew, so, too, did the range of powers attributed to him. He became known as the patron saint of wild birds and beasts in light of his reputation for having healed sick animals while a hermit. According to lore, he also applied his talent for healing to his fellow man. Presumptive relics of the saint were brought to western Europe by returning Crusaders, and as is the way with holy relics, these corporeal remnants proliferated in nothing less than near miraculous fashion.

18

Illustration 6: Blaise goes postal.

The Catholic feast of St. Blaise is February 3rd, February 11th for the Eastern Orthodox Church. In many places a blessing is given by placing two crossed candles, sometimes tied with a red ribbon symbolizing martyrdom, over the head or by touching the throat of the faithful, the priest speaking the following (or similar) words: 'Through the intercession of Saint Blaise, bishop and martyr, may God deliver you from every disease of the throat and from every other illness.' The candles (traditional or intertwined designer versions with handle and red ribbon) will have been blessed the previous day, Candlemas (the Feast of the Presentation of Jesus Christ). This practice dates from the 15th or 16th century and continues all across the globe with local variations. In some countries a ribbon will be worn around the throat for several days after the blessing; in my own childhood case, a penitential piece of rough red flannel was pinned under my shirt next to my skin, to be worn that day from morning 'til night. In a few cases, the faithful may be given the blessing with a bona fide relic of the saint. Often, the celebrations extend well beyond a simple blessing in a church to encompass full-blown religio-cultural festivals, and nowhere more so than in the historic city of Dubrovnik (illus.7).

Illustration 7: Postcards showing the Church of St. Blaise,
Dubrovnik and Cathedral of St. Blaise, St. Blasien, Germany.

21

BLAISE GOES GLOBAL

Churches named in honor of Saint Blaise are to be found all over the world, from Greece to Goa, the earliest dating from the 12th, 13th and 14th centuries. In France, Blaise is the patron of churches in, to take just a few examples at random, Arles, Dabo and Milly-la-Forêt, the last of which was decorated by Jean Cocteau and became his resting place. Of especial architectural note is the 12th-century Romanesque church in the village of L'Hôpital-Saint-Blaise in the south-west of the country, which has been listed as a UNESCO World Heritage Site. Across the English Channel, the Church of Saint Blaise in Haccombe-with-Combe in Devon was built around the 13th century. It is one of several so-called 'wool churches,' their construction having been financed in part or whole by fortunes made from the medieval wool trade. Typically, a wealthy patron would name a chapel or church after a favorite saint in the hope that he or she would act as an intercessor, improving their chances of salvation, of steering them clear of Purgatory and Hell. It was the instrument of Blaise's torture, a carding comb, that sealed the deal as far as the world of wool was concerned.

In Russia, where Blaise is known as Vlasiy, there are churches dating from as early the 12th century named in his honor, the photogenic, onion-domed gem in Veliky Novgorod being a good example (illus.8). In northern parts of the country, he was one of the most popular saints, particularly in his role as a protector of cattle. The saint also seems to have been regarded as a protector of draft-horses in wool-growing parts of Germany during the later Middle Ages; in Rothenburg, there is a small chapel named after him and a tradition of horses being blessed by the local priest and combs (a reference to his martyrdom) placed on the animals' heads. In Salzburg, Austria, the Kirche St.

23

Illustration 8: St. Blaise's Church, Veliky Novgorod, Russia.

Blasius sits on the site of a small 12th-century chapel originally named after the saint. Back in Germany, where he has long had a devoted following, the Lutheran church of St. Blaise in Hannoversch Münden dates from the end of the 13th century. In the Dom St. Blaisen (illus.7) in the town of St. Blasien there is a statue—that formerly stood in an Ursuline monastery in Vienna—of Blaise performing his most famous miracle; there is another of the miter-wearing saint on Cathedral Square. Somewhat improbably, Blaise also had a loyal following in Iceland and a reputation as a miracle worker during the Middle Ages. There existed several churches of which he was the patron or co-patron and these, typically, were located near water, be it open sea, a lake or river, an association which, it has been suggested, may relate to his miraculous walking on water and his intervention to save the life of the choking boy (illus.9).

In the village of Anento in Aragon, Spain (where Blaise translates as Blas) the single-nave Iglesia de San Blas is a 13th-century Romanesque jewel with a stunning Gothic altarpiece, at the center of which are images from the turbulent life of the saint. Other places of worship dedicated to Blas can be found in Villarrobledo, Salamanca, Ponferrada and La Palma. Across the border in Portugal, where San Blas translates as São Brás, his popularity is no less evident with many churches bearing his name, including those in Tavira and São Brás de Alportel (both in the Algarve). In Italy, dozens of villages, communes, churches, chapels and basilicas are named in honor of San Biagio, as he is known there. The city of Maratea is fiercely proud of its patron saint, with whom it has a centuries-long association. The local mountain is named after him, he has his own hymn (*Inno di San Biagio*, available on YouTube) and the Basilica di San Biagio holds remains of the martyred saint that are said to have been brought to the city in the eighth century by refugees fleeing from the iconoclasm of Leo III, the Byzantine emperor: their vessel was blown off course and made landfall at Maratea. In Montecatini Val di Cecina (near Pisa) stands the 14th-century Iglesia di San Biagio and in majestic Pisa Cathedral there is a 16th-century altar dedicated to Blaise. In

Montepulciano, the visitor will be delighted by the monumental Renaissance-style temple honoring the martyr while for those sightseeing in Rome the small Iglesia di San Biagio della Pagnotta (St. Blaise of the Loaf of Bread), today the national church of the city's Armenian community, is worth a visit for its paintings of the saint and a reliquary containing a throat fragment. In Catholic Ireland, by way of contrast, Blaise seems to have lost out to the 'Big Three' locals: Patrick, Brigid and Columcille. Although his feast day is widely acknowledged and the holy blessing administered in many churches on February 3rd, Blaise's name does not appear to have been bestowed on a single chapel, church, well, street, school or pub anywhere in the country. I confess to being slightly disappointed. Nonetheless, to compile an inventory of churches and chapels named after Saint Blaise across all of western Europe would be no mean undertaking; an almost impossible one if a truly global inventory were the goal.

Blaise's Luso-Hispanic popularity spread westwards as a result of 16th-century colonization and the subsequent partitioning of the Americas by Spain and Portugal. The proselytizing *conquistadores* imposed their faith on the indigenous populations, transplanting belief systems, traditions and hagiographies. Among the panoply of saints who established themselves in the New World was Blaise: São Brás in Portuguese-speaking Brazil, San Blas elsewhere. In Brazil, municipalities (São Brás de Suaçuí in the state of Minas Gerais), churches (Igreja Matriz São Brás in Paraí) and festivals (Festa São Brás in Trancoso in the beach state of Bahía) are named after the early martyr. In Paraguay, where Blas is considered by some the patron saint of the country, his feast day is celebrated widely, nowhere more so than in Itá, home to a 17th-century Franciscan church named in his honor.

Illustration 9: A children's book about St. Blaise.

The epicenter of the Blaise cult in Peru is the colonial city of Cusco, heart of the Inca empire until the Spanish conquest. Today it is the Historical Capital of the country and a UNESCO World Heritage Site. The 16th-century baroque Iglesia de San Blas, built over an Incan shrine, is located in the Barrio de San Blas. It is a major tourist attraction, featuring a unique carved wooden pulpit (made from a single tree trunk). Needless to say, Blas's feast day is celebrated in the neighborhood with much brio. One can travel all over Latin America and come across buildings, institutions, festivals or places named after the saint, but few will be as attractive as Bahía San Blaise (Saint Blaise's Bay) in Patagonia, also known as 'Fisherman's Paradise.' (For the record, Bahía San Blas is the name of a ship in the Argentine navy, something that might not meet with the irenic saint's full approval.) On Mexico's Pacific coast lies the 18th-century port of San Blas, a somewhat somnolent town that time has passed by but one that remains in the literary mind thanks to Longfellow's poem, *The Bells of San Blas*. It was the poet's last composition, written in March 1882, and describes a place he had never actually visited. Blaise's popularity in Central and South America persists, but waves of immigrants from Western Europe and the Slavic nations in particular have ensured that the martyr also has a strong presence in North America. In the US, you'll find churches named after him in Illinois, Massachusetts, Michigan and Pennsylvania and a street, Saint Blaise Lane, in Youngsville, Louisiana.

St. Blaise may have originated in Armenia and have a dedicated following all across the world (see illus.10), but the hypocenter of his cult is, arguably, Croatia, specifically the enchanting walled city of Dubrovnik, formerly known as Ragusa, a UNESCO World Heritage Site. (What is it about Blaise and UNESCO World Heritage Sites, I wonder?) The history of the miniature Republic of Ragusa is complicated but suffice it to say that during the 14th century it removed itself from the suzerainty of the Republic of Venice and became an autonomous city state and maritime trade rival of *La Serenissima*. Some Italians take umbrage at what they see as the appropriation of their saint by their Slav near neighbors, not least, one suspects, the residents of Maratea but, given the historic rivalry between Venice and Dubrovnik, it is hardly surprising. In fact, it is not in the least surprising. The very first mention of the inordinately popular saint dates from the 10th century (February 2nd, 971, to be specific) when, so the story goes, Blaise, dressed as an old man, and lurking in the church of Saint Stephen in Ragusa, introduced himself before issuing a warning to the local pastor, one Stojko, who happened upon him, having found the doors of the church unexpectedly left open. (Alternatively, the saint appeared to Stojko in a dream.) The galleys anchored beyond the city walls had come for reasons other than those assumed by the residents; the Venetians' true motive was a surprise attack on their pesky rival. Stojko duly informed the authorities. The city fathers heeded the mysterious warning. The city shut its gates and set to manning the massive defensive walls. With that show of force and realizing that their Trojan horse strategy had backfired, the fleet sailed off. Coincidentally, the warning had been received on the eve of Saint Blaise's day. The citizenry, as befitted the times, duly adopted the saint as their protector and patron. An unbreakable association was thus established.

The attentive first-time visitor to Dubrovnik will spot a large statue of the hallowed saint in full fig above the main gate into the old city. He's holding a maquette of the walled town in his left hand. Sveti Blaž—or Sveti Vlaho as he is referred to in the local dialect—is an almost palpable presence within the city's walls, his likeness omnipresent, his legend retold at the drop of a hat. He is revered to this day, in words and song (multiple versions of 'Oh, Sveti Vlaho' by Tereza Kesovija are available on YouTube) and the annual festival in his honor is one of, if not the biggest in the world. I confess I had been unaware of the historical ties between saint and city until my professional career took me in the mid-1980s to the Inter-University Center in Dubrovnik to co-organize a series of conferences with peers from the University of Zagreb (illus.11). I immediately felt at home, with both the people and the place. Sharing a name with the all-

29

important saint was an icebreaker, made me feel at ease with colleagues from all over what at the time was known as Yugoslavia. Maybe things would have worked out exactly the same if I had been baptized Trevor, but I suspect not. Since then, Dubrovnik, sadly, has suffered the same fate as Venice: mass tourism. But with blinkers and determination, there is still much to see and enjoy, including the baroque Church of St. Blaise on the main street (Stradun). It is not, however, the original structure; that, along with much else, was destroyed in the devastating earthquake of 1667, something that not even miracle-working Blaise could do a lot about. The church, with its statues of Blaise, inside and out, is a major attraction and its steps an ever-popular resting spot. But if you want to see priceless relics of the revered saint, then you'll need to head off to the treasury of Dubrovnik Cathedral.

What many locals but few tourists realize is that almost four thousand miles away a smaller though architecturally similar church, also dedicated to Saint Blaise, can be found in the village of Gandaulim, part of the former Portuguese colony of Goa (now India). The original Church of São Brás was built (possibly rebuilt) around about the middle of the 16th century by traders or shipbuilders from Dubrovnik, who went on to establish a small Croatian community on the edge of the Arabian Sea. The humble church is still there, still ministering to the needs of its parishioners and annually celebrating the feast day of São Brás with pride and devotion. As even a modest amount of digging around soon makes clear, Blaise's appeal transcends borders, cultures and eras. He really does seem to have near universal appeal. Funds permitting, you could take a relaxing break on the San Blas Islands off the Caribbean Coast or travel to Burundi for some R&R near Lake Tanganyika and there check into a three-star establishment named after the saint: the cheery Hotel St. Blaise even has a swimming pool.

Illustration 10: St. Blaise cards and prayer leaflets.

31

INTERNATIONAL CONFERENCE

INFORMATION RESOURCES
MANAGEMENT
concepts, strategies,
applications

Inter-University Centre of Postgraduate Studies
Dubrovnik, June 1-5, 1987

Referalni centar Sveučilišta u Zagrebu   University of Strathclyde

Illustration 11: Another stop on the conference circuit.

CELEBRATING BLAISE

It is quite remarkable how a third century Catholic martyr from Armenia has become the cynosure of worldwide celebrations every February. Of course, there is a solemn and reverential side to many of the festivities, but it would be disingenuous to suggest that Blaise doesn't also provide a good pretext for a knees-up. Nineteenth century Bradford is a case in point. As mentioned, the method of Blaise's torture tied him to the wool trade, to the trade's aristocracy in particular: wool-combers. As the textile industry boomed, Bradford prospered. The town adopted Blaise as its patron saint and in the early 19th century his feast day was celebrated every seventh year (beginning in 1811, if not earlier). But as skilled artisans were replaced gradually by machinery, the tradition died out. Local records do, however, convey a sense of the occasion: the colorful procession with wool-staplers, spinners, apprentices and merchants on horseback, the bright costumes and general merriment, including 'the Blaise Ball.' More recently, in 1931, the city held a Bishop Blaize (*sic*) Pageant (an official postcard depicts the larger-than-life, bearded, miter-wearing saint holding a crozier in his left hand and a wool comb in his right) and lately there have been attempts to revive the celebrations, with the help of Saint Blaise's Armenian Bitter, brewed by a local company.

One of the longest-running, liveliest and most colorful of festivals is that held annually in Bocairent, a picturesque hillside town located between Valencia and Alicante. It is all one would expect of Spain, where Sant Blai (as he is known locally) is celebrated with mass, peeling church bells, brass bands, processions and a froth of pageantry. His effigy and relic are trundled through the streets to shouted acclaim: '*Vitol al Patró Sant Blai.*' The fiesta runs for several days in early February, during which time the town's population more than doubles.

(Bocairent's website doesn't beat about the bush: 'From party to party, all year long,' it proclaims.) Not given to half measures, the locals combine their love of the saint with a reenactment of the historic battles between Moors and Christians, making this a two-for-the-price-of-one-festival. If it all proves too much, the overheated visitor can repair to the nearby *Cava de Sant Blai*, an enormous, sixteenth-century ice cave, a precursor of the modern fridge. But why Bocairent and Blaise? The association dates to the early 17th century when the town was stricken with an outbreak of diphtheria. The despairing inhabitants prayed to the saint, who, it seems, did the business. Thereupon, the grateful town adopted him as its patron, dumping poor Sant Jaume (Saint James) in the process.

From urban centers to villages all across the globe, Blaise's feast day is celebrated with spectacle and passion, from Ciudad del Este in Paraguay and Cusco in Peru to Valbonne in France and Maratea in Italy, where, by the way, there are two separate celebrations in his honor: the second taking place in May on the anniversary of the arrival, in a marble urn, of his relics into the city. Perhaps most impressive of all is how one saint has been coopted for so many different reasons by so many different constituencies in so many different places and celebrated in so many different ways, from cheese-rolling (*ruzzolone*) and bonfires in Italy to the scoffing, in Germany, of *Bubenschenkel* (fried bread in the shape of a boy's thighs). Given that Blaise is a saint about whom relatively little is known, it is astonishing how he has developed into such a protean talisman for so many people, in so many countries across the centuries. A cultural tourist could spend a lifetime following in the footsteps of Blaise, visiting the many places with which he has, or had, an association or following of one kind or another. Merely visiting the numerous churches named after him in Western Europe or attending all the festivals held annually in his honor in Italy alone would be a task sufficient to defeat even those blessed with Stakhanovite spirit.

Croats, of course, will claim that no other place on earth celebrates the saint's feast day with more passion than

Dubrovnik. The tradition dates back to the twelfth century and has grown into an elaborate multi-day affair combining ritual, pageantry, prayer, traditional craft activity and music. A measure of its significance is that the Festival of St. Blaise was added in 2009 to UNESCO's Representative List of the Intangible Cultural Heritage of Humanity. Dubrovnik is proprietorial about its protector but also proud to share his legacy with the wider world. The official proceedings begin on Candlemas when the flag of St. Blaise (white with a representation of the man himself, see illus.12) is raised in front of his church to cries of 'Long live Saint Blaise.' That triggers the ringing of church bells, musket fire, the release of white doves and the singing of vespers in the cathedral. The next day the 'city-wide bash,' to quote *Lonely Planet*, gets into top gear with bells and brass bands, along with the red-caped musketeers—*trombunjeri* as they are known—who make their own brief but unmistakable contribution to the soundtrack. Central elements of the colorful parade through the old town are priceless medieval reliquaries containing anatomical remains of the beloved saint, including his head, taken from the security of the *wunderkammer*-like cathedral treasury for this one day.

A cultural historian of food in search of a Ph.D. thesis topic could do worse than undertake an exploration of the significance of customs and ingredients associated with Blaise. His feast day makes clear how, all around the world, the patron saint of sore throats has become indelibly associated with certain types of food—tarts, cakes, sweets and, most commonly, blessed bread sticks (*pan bendito*, as approved in 1883 by the Congregation of Scared Rites). In different regions of Italy, you'll find, inter alia, *torta di San Biagio* (Lombardy, chocolate and almond pie), *panettone di San Biagio* (Milan, where the tradition is for the family to eat a stale Christmas *panettone* as a propitiatory gesture against illness of the throat), trachea-shaped *cannaruzzeddi di San Brasi* (Sicily), donut-shaped *taralli di San Biagio* (Abruzzo), *panicelle di San Biagio* (Abruzzo, bread in the shape of a four-fingered hand that purportedly represents the collective efforts of dyers, finishers, spinners and weavers in the wool industry),

35

polpette di San Biagio (Campania, meatballs), and *abbacolo di San Biagio* (Calabria, bread baked in the shape of a question mark or crozier and given by young men to their sweethearts, who, if they break it in two and hand one back are signaling a willingness to marry).

In the Basque country, where Saint Blaise is also a hugely popular figure and relics of the man abound, it is customary for the head of the household to bring apples, garlic and salt to church for blessing. These are later given to both children and animals for protection against all kinds of throat-related infections. Another food-related tradition is the blessing of wheat bread, enriched with butter, eggs, pepper and honey. A quirky variant on the theme is the blessing of pieces of cord, wrapped (in bygone times) around bread. For those who don't bake, a simple solution might be to buy two slender baguettes, cross them at your throat as if a pair of blessed candles, say a prayer, break off a chunk of bread and knock back a glass of red wine. These days, in Bilbao's Iglesia de San Nicolás the feast is celebrated with mass and the blessing of pieces of colored cotton cord with an image of the saint attached, on sale in the streets outside. Wearing the cord around one's neck for nine days after the blessing and then burning it should keep you free of tonsilitis, strep throat and such like. The festivities include a procession and the eating of marshmallows and pastries (*rosquillas*). Another traditional delicacy is the meringue-covered pastry known as *San Blas opila*, with the saint's name (or initials) inscribed on the top. In Campos, Mallorca, the feast day is celebrated with a mass at the Oratory of Saint Blaise and the eating of almond bread known as *panetets de Sant Blai*. One could go on.

Illustration 12: The flag of the Republic of Ragusa with St. Blaise.

BLAISE'S BITS AND BOBS

The Catholic Church has not, historically speaking, gone in for minimalism. From soaring spires and flying buttresses to gilded altar pieces and sanguinary statuary, the Vatican intuitively understood how architecture and decoration could awe and cow its flock. Nothing was done by halves, little left to chance. The stylistic excesses associated with Catholicism might appall most Muslims and Methodists, but as the old saw goes, nothing succeeds like excess. Holy mass was a form of theater, featuring luminous liturgical vestments, jewel-studded chalices, choral music, wafting incense and mystique—mummery in the eyes of some. The faithful prayed not only to Jesus, Mary and Joseph for help, but to an army of saints, whose intercession would be sought in countless ways on a daily basis. In the Middle Ages, the veneration of saints had become a defining feature of quotidian life. For the lowly and destitute as well as the educated and high-born, a favored saint would be prayed to in the hope of a miraculous intervention, be it protection against the plague or help finding a lost lamb. If prayers were answered, the beneficent saint might, in exceptional cases, have a chapel, school or church established in his or her honor. The power attributed by the faithful to saints would, naturally, be amplified as stories of miraculous cures or divine interventions were shared and embellished. Nothing boosted a saint's stock like a popularly acclaimed miracle.

The veneration of saints led to the collecting of relics: whole body parts, shards of bone, tufts of hair, fragments of clothing, or personal belongings, ranging from a manuscript to a walking cane. A relic, unlike a two or three-dimensional representation, is the physical instantiation of the departed soul. There is a direct link between the object of veneration and the subject, between the physical and spiritual realms. As such, these remnants are ascribed a potency that a painting, fresco or statute cannot possess. They serve a healing or apotropaic function. In short, they are held, by the credulous at any rate, to have magical properties. Unsurprisingly, demand for relics exploded, creating an extensive market in saintly remains, among both institutions and individuals. And as so often is the case when demand outstrips supply, the temptation to create knockoffs can prove hard to resist. What holds today in the fine art and luxury goods sectors held in medieval times in respect of relics. In 1543 John Calvin wrote a scorching pamphlet on the subject (*Traité des Reliques*), mocking those who ascribed supernatural power to bodily bits and pieces, moreover bits and pieces of often dubious provenance. Given the number of churches claiming to have a piece of the True Cross on which Jesus was crucified, he estimated that there would be enough wood to build a ship. In fairness, it should be pointed out that in 1870 a well-known French architect, Charles Rohault de Fleury, specifically addressed this issue in his *Mémoire sur les instruments de la Passion de N.S. Jésus-Christ.* Having sedulously catalogued all known relics of the True Cross and having estimated the likely size and mass of said cross, he concluded, to the Church's undoubted relief, that, in fact, most of the cross actually remained unaccounted for. Be that as it may, it does not require much rootling around to discover that—miraculously—quite a few saints were born with more than one head and with multiple arms and legs, Blaise included.

Relics may be anathema to iconoclasts, but there is still a healthy appetite for saintly remnants among Catholics and, of course, antiquarians. To this day they retain their appeal, even if the faithful are perhaps not quite as superstitious as once was the case. And it's not just the Old World that has an enduring love affair with holy relics. In Pittsburgh—birthplace of image-maker extraordinaire Andy Warhol—St. Anthony's Chapel has a breathtaking collection of more than 5,000 specimens contained in some 800 reliquaries, the legacy of an obsessive Belgian-born collector, the church's 'priest-physician,' Father Suitbert Godfrey Mollinger. Outside the Vatican, it is the largest collection of relics in the world but it's not the only place in the US where you'll find a bit of Blaise. A few years ago, the Cathedral of the Sacred Heart in Pueblo, Colorado, announced that it had acquired a first-class relic (i.e., body part) of the saint, a piece of his left femur bone to be precise. Calvin's protestations, one has to say, were not entirely without foundation. The antique postcard reproduced here (illus.13) captures the absurdity of polycephalic saints by caricaturing the unfortunate Blaise, but he was far from the only holy man to have more limbs than was humanly possibly nor even the most prodigiously gifted when it came to supernumerary limbs. Unlike with paintings, where experts and connoisseurs can make attributions with considerable confidence, verifying the remnants of saints is an impracticable task, given the lack of empirical and documentary evidence. So much needs to be taken on trust. Moreover, which church, museum or individual collector is going to concede that this or that relic is anything other than one hundred percent genuine?

There isn't the remotest possibility that Dubrovnik's head, arm and hand of Blaise, housed in priceless reliquaries, are ever going to admit challenge, be downgraded or de-accessioned. And it is inconceivable that the citizens of Maratea could ever imagine that their prized fragments were anything other than genuine. Nor is there any likelihood that the clergy of Braunschweig might question the authenticity of their wood and gilt, ring-bedizened reliquary containing Blaise's arm any more than the congregation of Iglesi di Carlo ai Catinari in Rome might doubt the provenance of their precious throat bone. That the sum of Blaise's parts is likely greater than the whole is of no consequence to most believers. Counting the number of angels on a pinhead or totting up all the arms and legs belonging to Blaise housed in Catholic churches and Orthodox monasteries are activities best left to pedants and killjoys. In the case of relics, believing is seeing.

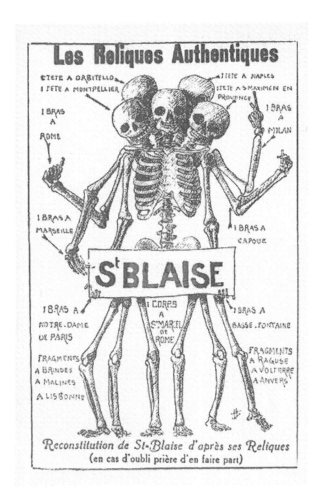

Illustration 13: Antique French postcard, Les Reliques Authentiques.

REPRESENTATIONS OF BLAISE

Even if all Blaise's extant body parts could be collocated and painstakingly reassembled, we would still struggle to come up with a highly credible likeness of the third-century saint, though forensic facial reconstruction technology might help. That, however, has not deterred artists from giving free rein to their imagination. There are innumerable extant representations of St. Blaise spanning the centuries, which is not surprising: he was, in the Middle Ages, an extremely popular figure and, at that time, images of saints abounded, in churches, chapels, monasteries and the abodes of the wealthy. In terms of his physique and physiognomy, even a casual perusal of publicly available art-historical images confirms the lack of consensus as to what he looked like, bar the near ubiquitous beard. But that is probably true for most of the older saints—think of the human pin cushion, Sebastian, another enduringly popular, early Church martyr, who, despite being depicted as relatively youthful and mostly clean shaven, never looks the same from one rendition to the next.

Artistic license notwithstanding, there exists a clearly recognizable iconography of St. Blaise. He is typically portrayed in a small number of ways, his life and virtues symbolized using an established set of tropes. Most commonly, the saint is shown wearing a chasuble and crozier and holding a miter, as in Bicci di Lorenzo's rather prosaic 15th-century painting of the seated bishop in the Indianapolis Museum of Art. Sometimes in his other hand he has a candle (or two) alluding to his most famous miracle. Alternatively, as in the case of the statue in Bradford's Wool Exchange, he holds only the carding iron. In the 15th-century panel by Neri di Bicci (Yale University) reproduced here (illus.14) he holds both a crozier and wool comb.

Illustration 14: 'Virgin and Child Enthroned with Saints Martin of Tours and Blaise' by Neri di Bicci.

The statue of Blaise atop his church in Dubrovnik depicts him with gold crozier and miter. Inside the building, above the altar, is a 15th-century silver gilt statue of the protector, again holding a model of the city in his hand. This iconic piece survived the great earthquake. In the Basilica di San Biagio in Maratea, the much-venerated effigy of Blaise shows him giving a blessing with his right hand while holding both a crozier and wool comb in his left. Frequently, Blaise will be seen wearing red, symbolizing martyrdom. At other times, in place of either the candle or crozier, he will be holding a wood and metal wool comb, signifying his torture. The British Library has a beautiful 12th-century cover of an illuminated manuscript with Blaise in full regalia gripping both a crozier and fearsome-looking comb. Reinforcing the symbolism is a lamb next to his feet. In the altarpiece of the Church of Saint Blaise in Anento (Spain) he is wearing an ornate crown and wrapped in a stunning, full-length carmine robe, this time holding a comb along with a codex. Iconic depictions of the Hieromartyr Blaise in the Orthodox Church are more conformist in terms of style, typically showing him handling a jewel-studded codex (see illus.15).

Blaise's martyrdom has long been a favorite subject for artists, with considerable variation in both painterly style and imagery. In Allegretto Nuzi's 14th-century panel (Yale University) the Bishop of Sebaste is shown on his knees about to be decapitated, the dead bodies of other contemporaneous martyrs in the foreground. A notably vigorous depiction of Blaise's gory end is Mariotto di Nardo's 15th-century 'The Martyrdom of Saint Blaise' (Musée des Beaux-Arts de Rennes) that shows him draped on a crucifix, tied by hand and foot rather than nailed. He is wearing a loin cloth and miter. To his left and right, his tormentors are shown hacking at his torso with wool combs. A variation on this theme is provided by Giovanni Antonio da Pesaro's 15th-century painting (Museo Nazionale del Palazzo di Venezia, Rome) which has Blaise brutalized by two comb-welding lackies of the emperor. Gaspar de Crayer's 17th-century version of the event (St. Martin, Zaventem, The Netherlands, illus.16) depicts Blaise suspended by the wrists, his

*Illustration 15: 'St. Blaise of Sebaste.' Anonymous.
Late 17th-century Russian icon.*

*Illustration 16: 'Martyrdom of Saint Blaise'
by Gaspar de Crayer.*

torturers at hand with their flaying instruments.

Another approach has been to portray Blaise in quotidian scenes, particularly surrounded by, communing with or healing animals. In this 15th-century Russian icon (illus.17) he is shown with a number of stylized, horned animals, while in Sano di Pietro's 15th-century rendition, 'Saint Blaise is fed by the birds' (Pinacoteca Nazionale, Siena), he is dressed in religious garb and standing outside his cave with more than a dozen solicitous birds. 'St. Blaise preaching to the animals' is a bucolic 16th-century Tyrolean School picture (private collection) that shows the saint sitting in the countryside, dressed, incongruously, in episcopal garb, at ease with an attentive audience of birds and animals, both domestic and wild. In popular art, from cheap icons and prayer cards to retablos and medals, he is often shown as a friend and healer of the four-legged.

Yet another component of the iconography of St. Blaise are his miraculous interventions in the lives of Sebaste's appreciative citizens. The miracle of the wolf returning the piglet unharmed to the woman is captured in Sano di Pietro's 15th-century painting, 'Saint Blaise commanding the wolf to give the pig back to the poor widow' (Pinacoteca Nazionale, Siena). In the top left quadrant, we see the widow begging for Blaise's help; in the foreground we see the docile wolf approaching the grateful woman, the curly tailed pig, unharmed, clasped between its teeth. A richly painted, French four-panel illuminated manuscript dating from the 14th century (Vatican Library) shows the red-robed saint: (i) with animals, (ii) extracting the fishbone from the boy, (iii) instructing the wolf to return the pig, and (iv) holding steel combs. If a single work of art can summarize the life of Blaise, this, surely, is it. Tucked away in the Vatican Library, it will be seen by few.

Illustration 17: Saint Blaise with animals. Anonymous.
15th-century Russian icon.

CODA

During my primary school days, I became a mite self-conscious about my given name, sometimes wished I'd been called John or Paul. But my mother had determined that her brood would be blessed (or burdened) with exotic names, exotic, that is, by the standards of 1950s Ireland. Not that I was ridiculed or bullied. At no time did I acquire a nickname: neither Blazer nor Blaisy ever caught on, nor any other derivative. Perhaps the fact that the saint's feast day was celebrated in the local Dominican church had a legitimizing effect. As a consequence, in parochial Newry—if not indeed Ulster—I remained a singleton until my late teens when my sister introduced me to another Blaise, a young male friend of hers. I remember the moment well, the dudgeon I experienced on meeting the whippersnapper, but I masked my puerility. So, I *was* proprietorial about my name after all. I really didn't want to share it with others. Today, truth be told, I'd probably bridle if introduced to a female Blaise.

With time I came to realize that the name's relative rarity was, on balance, a positive thing, particularly since my family name was far from unusual. In the US, when I introduce myself, it continues, more often than not, to be a case of 'Come again?' As far as spelling goes, the default is Blaze—certainly in Starbucks (illus.17)—which may be down to Blaze Starr, the famous Louisiana stripper ('The Hottest Blaze in Burlesque') who had a high-profile affair in the 1950s with the state's governor, Earl Long. Very occasionally (even in print) it's Blasé, which is how one of my neighbors in the west of Ireland calls me despite my best efforts to correct his pronunciation. In letters and emails, I am still more likely to be addressed as Ms. than Mr. Cronin by people who are unacquainted with me. As far as my academic career goes, I'd have to say that being a Blaise rather than a John has been a plus, hard though it might be to quantify the benefits.

51

If nothing else, an author called Blaise is more likely to stand out than one called John. Or so I choose to think. Perhaps it's time to write my swansong: 'The bibliographic benefits of being baptized Blaise.' I would, of course, dedicate the piece to the Armenian bishop about whom we know so little but around whom we have woven so much. At the very least, those of us trading under his name owe it to the sainted martyr to acknowledge the gift he unwittingly gave us.

Illus. 18: Starbucks siren and Blaze.

Image Credits

Cover photo (and illus.15): Detail from a late 17th-century Russian icon depicting St. Blaise of Sebaste. Collection of the author.

Illus.2: Kerry Hood. Available at:
https://commons.wikimedia.org/wiki/File:2014feb15_4578_st_blaises_well_palace-park.jpg

Illus.4: Art Institute of Chicago. Available at:
https://commons.wikimedia.org/wiki/File:Antonio_Molleno_-_Saint_Blasius_-_1975.174_-_Art_Institute_of_Chicago.jpg

Illus.5: Jastrow. Available at:
https://commons.wikimedia.org/wiki/File:Saint_Blaise_Louvre_OAR504.jpg

Illus. 8: Alaexis. Available at:
https://commons.wikimedia.org/wiki/File:St._Blasius_church,_Novgorod.JPG

Illus.12: Berto456. Available at:
https://commons.wikimedia.org/wiki/File:St._Blaise_-_National_Flag_of_the_Ragusan_Republic.png

Illus.13: Public domain. Available at:
https://commons.wikimedia.org/wiki/File:Carte_Postale_%E2%80%9CLes_Reliques_Authentiques%E2%80%9D.jpg

Illus.14: Courtesy of Yale University Art Gallery.

Illus.16: Public domain. Available at:
https://commons.wikimedia.org/wiki/File:Gaspar_de_Crayer_-_Martyrdom_of_Saint_Blaise.jpg

Illus.17: Public domain. Available at:
https://commons.wikimedia.org/wiki/File:Saint_Blaise_and_animals_2.jpg

About the Author

Photo: The author, Church of St. Blaise, Dubrovnik, 1984.

Blaise Cronin, Rudy Professor Emeritus of Information Science at Indiana University, divides his time between Bloomington and Westport, Ireland. Born in Newry, he was educated at Trinity College Dublin and Queen's University Belfast.

Printed in Great Britain
by Amazon

77117968R10036